LEGAL FEASTS

LEGAL FEASTS

M.H. HOEFLICH

TALBOT
PUBLISHING
Clark, New Jersey

ISBN 978-1-61619-688-2

TALBOT PUBLISHING

AN IMPRINT OF
THE LAWBOOK EXCHANGE, LTD.
33 Terminal Avenue
Clark, New Jersey 07066-1321

Please see our website for a selection of our other publications and fine facsimile reprints of classic works of legal history:
www.lawbookexchange.com

Library of Congress Cataloging-in-Publication Data

Names: Hoeflich, Michael H., author.
Title: Legal feasts / M.H. Hoeflich.
Description: First edition. | Clark : Talbot Publishing, an Imprint of The Lawbook Exchange, Ltd., 2024. | Includes bibliographical references. | Summary: "An illustrated collection of essays, reproduced menus, and recipes relating to the history of commensal and convivial dining in the legal profession"-- Provided by publisher.
Identifiers: LCCN 2023054830 | ISBN 9781616196882 (paperback)
Subjects: LCSH: Lawyers--Social life and customs--History. | Dinners and dining--History. | Menus. | Fasts and feasts--History.
Classification: LCC K117 .H64 2024 | DDC 394.1/2508834--dc23/eng/20231201
LC record available at https://lccn.loc.gov/2023054830

Printed in the United States of America on acid-free paper

To Yolanda Huggins for all her help and support for so many years, this small chapbook is dedicated.

SECTION I:
Conviviality & Commensality

Throughout my four decades as a lawyer, law professor, and law school dean, I have attended hundreds of receptions, dinners, casual get-togethers, and other professional events, almost all of which involved some form of snacks, meals, buffet, drinks, or some combination thereof. Many of these were quite elaborate and were splendid convivial events.[1] When I was a dean, I often found myself attending multiple events in a single day, all with some form of food and drink, as a result of which my waistline grew quite large. Looking back on these various events and the culinary and vinous delights served therein, I have come to realize that one particularly important aspect of the lawyerly life is and always has been convivial meals and communal gatherings. This is how we bond as professionals and create professional networks. I suspect that the general public might well be surprised that a profession dedicated to adversarial activities can, after hours, be so convivial.

While legal literature is full of narrative accounts of such communal activities going back to the earliest days of the Bar, the material remains of these meals and entertainments are far less common. Narrative histories can only go so far to help us understand these events. The material remains of these meals, however, the menus and illustrations that accompanied them, add an extra dimension. The rarity of these remains of often splendid and extravagant feasts is a result of the fact that they have been classified as ephemera by libraries and many booksellers. The very term ephemera hints at their fate.

---

1 This introductory essay is dedicated to my late friend, fellow gourmand, and colleague, James Smoot, Esq., with whom I had the privilege to help plan the Cravath dinner, the menu from which appears later in this book. It is my hope that now he dines in a celestial banquet hall. The essay itself is drawn heavily from M.H. Hoeflich, *Conviviality and Commensality at the Bar: History, Images, and Menus*, 25 GREEN BAG 205 (2022).

Libraries have long defined themselves as repositories of the textual memories of civilization and have tended to restrict these textual artifacts to books in manuscript or printed form.[2] Ephemeral texts, which, by their very nature, were not intended to be preserved over a long period of time, have rarely come within librarians' definition of artifacts worthy of being preserved. If they are to be preserved at all it is by museums or private collections, not institutional libraries.

∾

In the Anglo-American legal tradition, communal meals and entertainments date back at least to the Inns of Court in the early modern period. Barristers lived, worked, dined, and played in the Inns and there were multiple opportunities for convivial dining, from ordinary dinners to grand feasts and revels. Feasts were frequent, especially on the admission of a new member to the profession and on occasions when a lawyer delivered a "reading" before an Inn's members.

Professor Wilfred Prest, one of the greatest historians of the early modern English Bar, has studied Readers' dinners at the early modern Inns and provided a remarkable narrative of the gluttony that often accompanied these events.[3] The variety, quantity, and cost of the foods served boggles the modern mind. One imagines a seemingly endless parade of platters of meats and sweets presented to the diners along with copious quantities of ale, wine, and brandy. It is not at all surprising that by all accounts these were, indeed, loud, boisterous, and

---

2 Today, of course, libraries take a far broader view of their mission and preserve information in virtually all media. However, very few preserve ephemeral printed materials to this day.

3 Wilfrid Prest, *Readers' Dinners and the Culture of the Early Modern Inns of Court, in* THE INTELLECTUAL AND CULTURAL WORLD OF THE EARLY MODERN INNS OF COURT 107–123 (Jayne Archer, Elizabeth Goldring, and Sarah Knight ed., 2011); *see also,* PAUL RAFFIELD, IMAGES AND CULTURES OF LAW IN EARLY MODERN ENGLAND 9–42 (2004).

convivial affairs. In fact, such excessive banquets were not exclusive to lawyers. The monarchies and aristocracies of the Middle Ages and Early Modern era saw communal banqueting as one of the legacies of the Roman empire and a means by which to display their wealth, standing, and power to their peers and to the populace. Some, like the Duke of Ferrara, published the menus from banquets which they had hosted. Manuals on how to put on such displays of culinary excess were common.

Communal banquets have played many roles in our civilization. They often commemorate significant historical events. They may also commemorate an important person, one who is visiting a new place or one who is undergoing a life-changing event such as a marriage or retirement. The visit of Charles Dickens to Boston, for instance, was commemorated by a massive banquet. Graduations are often accompanied by communal meals, in public or in private. Even death brings people together to share food and drink, as in the Irish tradition of the wake and the Jewish tradition of *shiva*. Food and communal dining are quintessentially human.

Professor Peter Goodrich has studied these occasions and has suggested that these dinners served several specific professional purposes for members of the Bar.[4] They were, above all, "male bonding" events. Early modern lawyers, as noted, lived, worked, dined, and played together within a small physical space in London. Such bonding within each Inn and within the profession as a whole meant that the legal profession could exercise informal social control of its

---

4 Peter Goodrich, *Eating Law: Commons, Common Land, Common Law*, 12 J. OF LEGAL HISTORY 246, 246 (1991); *see also* RAFFIELD, *supra* note 3, at 9–42, particularly at 16–22 where Professor Raffield argues for the connection between culinary practices at the early modern Inns of Court and such practices at medieval monasteries.

members and function as a collective body, much the way that the colleges of Oxford and Cambridge functioned, themselves based on the model of monastic communities. These events were also opportunities to demonstrate the wealth and social standing of the lawyer hosts and, thereby, increase their status amongst their peers and their clients. In this way they were also philanthropic events, with gifting of food and drink from wealthier lawyers to those less blessed, an essential component of acquiring status within the Inns. They were an effective means of creating strong personal as well as professional networks. They were also, by most accounts, quite fun.

The tradition of commensality and conviviality at the Bar continued in England and was brought to the United States. One of the earliest attempts to form a bar association in Massachusetts was the creation of a lawyers' group, named by its founders, the *Sodalitas*, the Roman term for a drinking society. Ann Fidler, in her brilliant doctoral dissertation, *Young Limbs of the Law*, speaks of the importance of law students and apprentices dining together as a means of socializing young lawyers to the traditions and ethics of the Bar in antebellum America. These dinners and gatherings were a way of older, more experienced lawyers informally mixing with and teaching younger lawyers behaviors that might not have been so easily conveyed in the courthouse. Professor Goodrich points out, as does Maxwell Bloomfield, that the general public often criticized lawyers for gluttony and excessive drinking at such affairs, not understanding the critical subtexts of such events.[5]

Law student and lawyer diaries demonstrate the importance of eating and drinking communally, particularly with other lawyers. During his apprenticeship with Theophilus Parsons,

---

5 CHRISTINE ANN FIDLER, "YOUNG LIMBS OF THE LAW": LAW STUDENTS, LEGAL EDUCATION, AND THE OCCUPATIONAL CULTURE OF ATTORNEYS, 1820–1860 (1996); MAXWELL BLOOMFIELD, AMERICAN LAWYERS IN A CHANGING SOCIETY (1976).

John Quincy Adams maintained a detailed daily diary. The diary is filled with accounts of dinners with other lawyers taking place on special occasions as well as spontaneously. Adams paid particular attention in his entries to the quality of the food and drink as well as to post-prandial entertainments such as singing and cards. He especially prized dinners with his master because these provided him an opportunity to speak with and impress the elder lawyer.

Of course, in England, the Inns of Court and the Law Society continued—and continue to this day—to stress the importance of commensality in their communal dinners. Indeed, as Professor Goodrich comments, it is hard to identify many places in which communal dining a certain number of times is a professional requirement. The tradition of such commensality and conviviality extended beyond law schools in nineteenth-century America and, happily, to today.

Such convivial meals were common not only in urban centers, but also on country circuits. Perhaps the best account of non-urban convivial lawyer meals and other entertainments may be found in Henry Whitney's classic *Life on the Circuit with Lincoln.*[6] Lincoln and Whitney travelled the Eighth Judicial Circuit in Illinois together from 1854 to 1858. The presiding circuit judge was Lincoln's friend, David Davis, an immensely sociable—and gluttonous—man.[7] The lawyers would travel together, sleep in the same hostelry together, and dine and party together under the leadership of Judge Davis.[8]

---

6 HENRY CLAY WHITNEY, LIFE ON THE CIRCUIT WITH LINCOLN 61–88 (rev. ed. 1940).

7 Photographs of Judge Davis clearly betray a fondness for food; *see The Lawyers: David Davis (1815–1886)*, MR. LINCOLN AND FRIENDS, "Mr. Lincoln and Friends," http://www.mrlincolnandfriends.org/the-lawyers/david-davis/.

8 And, on occasion when accommodations were in short supply, even sleep together.

This ensured the development of a camaraderie among the lawyers that made the long days of travel and the difficult conditions they experienced bearable. Life on the circuits in England, though less primitive than in the American West, was equally convivial, filled with splendid meals, and created a similar *esprit du corps*.

Over the past century, the importance of social events at the Bar, particularly communal and celebratory dinners, has not diminished. Law schools, bar associations, law clubs, and other groups of lawyers delight in holding dinners and banquets, often featuring extensive bills of fare and multiple speakers. In the following illustrations of the material remains of these events we may, like nineteenth century antiquarians and modern-day archaeologists of ancient empires, learn much about an important aspect of past lawyers' lives.

SECTION II:
Menus

Of all legal dining ephemera, printed menus are the most common.[9] They vary significantly in terms of quality of printing, illustrations, if any, contents other than a list of food and drink served, and in the quality and quantity of the selections of food and drink. Often they list a program of speakers and honorees. The contents vary to a large extent based upon the event itself, the purpose for the event, and the wealth of those who paid for the event. Generally, one can say that when lawyers get together to dine, they like to dine well. The menus contained in this book date from the nineteenth and twentieth centuries and are from the United States with, as a comparison, three remarkable examples from Scotland and England. They run the gamut from fairly modest affairs to extraordinarily lavish events.

Menus of special banquets are more than just guides to a dinner. They are memorials to a noteworthy occasion. They are not simply texts; they are artifacts because they are often embellished with artwork relevant to the group giving the banquet or to the honoree. They are often quite beautiful and art in their own right. They also often contain lists of attendees, lists that let us understand social and professional networks. There are also programs included in many that list speakers, toasts, even songs to be sung at the appropriate moment. The language of the menus themselves are significant because language often indicates the social status and aspirations of those giving the banquet and those attending it. And, of course, the choice of dishes also is a strong indicator of the social

---

9 See, Grolier Club, *A Century of Dining Out. The American Story in Menus, 1841–1941* (2023). Henry Voight, from whose collection this exhibition was mounted, is the foremost collector of and expert about menus in the United States.

importance and economic status of the hosts, the honorees, and the attendees.

One especially interesting aspect of the menus and the meals described in this book is the extensive use of French to describe the food offerings at several of these legal feasts. Professor Paul Freedman, of Yale, one of the most distinguished food historians in the United States, has written about the use of French to describe dishes in the U.S.[10] Fundamentally, by the middle of the nineteenth century, French cuisine had become elite cuisine and was seen as more refined and sophisticated than home-grown dishes. Indeed, many dishes that had their origins in clearly local culinary traditions, like turtle soup, appeared dressed in French garb on menus at expensive restaurants and banquets. We may fairly surmise that the use of French and "Frenchified" dishes on banquet menus illustrated the desire not only to emphasize the prestige of the event, but, also, to reflect the growing gallicization of American cooking. Indeed, many of the dishes listed in the menus in French were quite simple and were not French at all. Sirloin steak and poached salmon were good hearty Anglo-American fare, even if clothed in French titles.

10 Paul Freedman, *The Rhetoric of American Restaurant Menus and the Use of French, in* FOOD AND LANGUAGE 129–136 (Richard Hosking ed., 2010).

THE FEASTS

The menus have been selected to provide a representation of law-related banquets from the late nineteenth until the late twentieth century. They have been arranged chronologically. They vary enormously in terms of the quantity and quality of the food, the importance of the event, the typography of the menus themselves, and the contents of the menu (such as a program or list of speakers). Some list the wines that accompanied the meals; others are silent as to what was drunk.

Menu.

Huîtres.	Bière Noire. Chablis.
Tortue Claire. Purée à la Palesti.	Amontillado.
Turbot, Sauce de Homard.	
Eperlans frits.	
Kromeskis de Foie Gras à la Perigueux.	E. Irroy et Cie.
Côtelettes de Mouton aux Marrons.	Carte d'Or. 1884.
Aloyau de Bœuf rôti au crème de Raifort.	
Dinde bouilli, Sauce Celeri.	
Jambon de York braisé.	
Faisans. Canards Sauvages.	Do.
Pouding à la Saxon.	
Gelée au Marasquin. Compôte de Poires.	
Croûtes aux Sardines Ecossaises fumets.	
Dessert.	Amontillado.
Crème au pain brun à la Vanille.	Cos d'Estournel. 1875.
Eau d'Oranges.	Liqueurs.
Thé et Café.	

Retirement Dinner by
the Bar of Scotland for Lord Shand
1890

The Scots Bar is a small, closely-knit group that values ceremony. On 1 November 1890, the Bar held a dinner in honor of Lord Shand upon his retirement from the Bench. Judging by the menu and the entertainment, it was quite an evening. The menu was entirely in French, both a sign of the historically close relations between Scotland and France and the status of French food in the later nineteenth century. The amount of food served is quite remarkable, as was the luxury of some of the dishes served: foie gras, mutton, beef, ham, turkey, wild duck, pheasant, and more. The meal was accompanied by toasts to the Queen, the Prince and Princess of Wales, the military, Parliament, and to the guest of honor. In addition, there were extensive musical selections played by "Mr. Laubach's band." The diners drank Amontillado Sherry, 1875 Cos D'Estournel, champagne (Irroy & Cie. Carte D'Or, 1884), and liqueurs. The menu itself is a work of art with illustrations including a wonderful caricature of the Scots Bar portrayed as an orchestra.

𝕸 𝖊 𝖓 𝖚.

Huîtres.

Consommé Parfait.
Crême à la Palestine.

Saumon aux Concombres.
Eperlans frites à la Diable.

Petits Bouchés à la Reine.
Ris de Veau glacée Financière.

Quartier d'Agneau—Sauce Menthe.
Petits Pois nouveaux.
Pommes nouvelles à la Pelûche.

Canards Sauvages et Poulets de Printemps.
Salade à la Française.

Asperges en branches.

Pouding Soufflé aux Pommes.
Gelée aux Liqueurs.

Croûtes de Champignons.

Glaçes et Dessert.

19th March.
CENTRAL HOTEL—J. GRANT, *Proprietor.*

Dinner for William Kirk Dickson
1897

The dinner held on the 19th of March, 1897 in honor of William Kirk Dickson, a prominent Scottish lawyer, followed the elegant tradition of the Shand dinner and featured both an artistic menu cover and a feast for the attendees.

Not surprisingly for a Scots legal feast, all of the dishes are named in French. But the food itself is of a definitely Scottish nature: oysters, salmon, lamb in mint sauce, duck. Perhaps the most notable aspect of this 1897 legal feast is the amount of food and the variety of the dishes. The guests were served ten courses. It is quite hard to imagine anyone going home hungry that night.

M E N U

OLIVES   CELERY   SALTED ALMONDS

BAKED WHITEFISH   MASHED POTATOES

FRENCH PEAS

BROWNED REED-BIRD   ORANGE SHERBET

SLICED CUCUMBERS SWEETBREAD CROQUETTES

STRAWBERRIES   ICE CREAM

WHITE CAKE   NABISCO WAFERS

ORANGES   BANANAS   HUYLER'S MINTS

COFFEE AND CREAM

BREAD   BUTTER

Darke County Bar Association
1903

The dinner memorialized in this menu was double-barreled, celebrating the retirement of one judge and the accession to the bench of another. It took place in a hotel in Greenville, Ohio, the county seat of Darke County, a small county on the border with Indiana.

Of the menus reprinted here, this menu from 1903 Ohio may well be the most unpretentious. The food is, for the most part, solidly midwestern. The main dishes, reed bird and sweetbread croquettes, will seem a bit odd to most modern readers, but they would have both been locally available. The baked whitefish would have been a familiar dish to the diners as well. What is, perhaps, most interesting is the identification of the wafers and mints by their brand, Nabisco and Huyler's. Presumably this would have impressed the diners. No drinks are listed, but we may hope that there were appropriate, if simple, potables offered as well.

ANNUAL DINNER

RHODE ISLAND BAR ASSOCIATION

THE ELOISE

PROVIDENCE, DECEMBER 4, 1911

Oysters   From Point Judith Pond

Radishes   Olives   Celery   Almonds

Apollinaris

Soup   Chicken Gumbo

Bread Sticks

Santerne Cup

Fish   Boiled Fresh Salmon

Hollandaise Potatoes   Cucumbers

Champagne

Entrée   Roast Philadelphia Capon, Chestnut Dressing   Pol Roger

Braised Potatoes   Fried Egg Plant   Cuvée de
Réserve

Sorbet   Punch Maraschino   Extra Dry
1900

Roast   Venison, Cumberland Sauce

Hominy Croquettes   Cigarettes

Salad   Tomato, Waldorf

Dessert   Bisque Tortoni

Fancy Cakes

Cheese   Roquefort   Camembert

Toasted Crackers

Coffee   Café Noir   Cigars

Annual Dinner of the
Rhode Island Bar Association
1911

The dinner provided to the members of the Rhode Island Bar Association in December 1911 looked both to local foods and American culinary favorites. There were oysters, chicken gumbo, fresh capon, venison, and fresh salmon. A bit of a foreign note was played with French cheese and an Italian dessert. The food was accompanied by a sauternes cup and Pol Roger champagne, as well as Apollinaris water and both cigarettes during the meal and cigars at the end. The menu itself is quite simply printed and speaks of solidity, as does the choice of food and drink.

LOWELL LAW CLUB.

1914

Lord Mansfield.

MENU

Oyster Cocktail

Mock Turtle, Baltimore
Olives   Radishes   Salted Nuts

Fried Smelts, Tarter Sauce
Cucumbers

Roast Duckling, Apple Sauce
Mashed Potatoes   String Beans

Cutlet of Sweetbread, Parisienne

Neapolitan Ice Cream
Assorted Cakes

Cheese   Crackers
Coffee

The Lowell Law Club Dinner
1914

One of the most important practice-oriented law school activities is—and has been—moot court.[11] At Harvard Law School, students were traditionally organized into "law clubs" named after legal notables, in which they competed in moot court proceedings. They also held club banquets. This menu was produced for the Lowell Law Club dinner in 1914.

The menu is illustrated with a portrait of Lord Mansfield, exemplifying, perhaps, Harvard Law's Anglophile inclinations at that time.[12] The dishes served were both abundant and quite posh, worthy of the young would-be lawyers who enjoyed them. Indeed, the parallels to dinners at the Inns of Court are unmistakable. Also notable is the presence of both oysters and mock turtle soup on the menu. As Paul Freedman has noted in his book, *Why Food Matters,* raw oysters and turtle were immensely popular dishes in the nineteenth and early twentieth century and were understood to be symbolic of luxury and wealth.[13] The inclusion of "sweet breads, *Parisienne*" is also a nod to luxury and elite status, since, at the time, French cuisine was considered to be the *ne plus ultra* of a dining experience. In other words, the elitist aspects of the Lowell Club menu would have been apparent to all who viewed it, precisely what the members desired.

---

11 *See* M.H. Hoeflich, *Plus ça Change, Plus c'est la Meme Chose: The Integration of Theory & Practice in Legal Education*, 66 TEMPLE L. REV., 123 (1993).

12 One should not overlook that Langdell in his *Cases on Contract* included virtually no American decisions.

13 PAUL FREEDMAN, WHY FOOD MATTERS 133–34 (2021).

MENU

Grape Fruit, Maraschino Cherries

Cream of Asparagus

Olives   Celery   Salted Nuts

Planked Shad, Manhattan

Noisette of Lamb, Cheron
Potatoes Rissolees

Roman Punch

Braised Capon au Jus

Salad in Season

Fresh Strawberry Ice Cream
Assorted Cakes

Coffee

Women Lawyers' Association Dinner
1914

By 1914 the Bar was no longer an exclusively male preserve and women lawyers quickly recognized the need both for their own bar associations and the value of commensality and conviviality for women lawyers. On 25 April 1914, the Woman Lawyers' Association held a dinner at the Hotel Manhattan in New York City. The menu served was a bit less elaborate (and less pretentious than the Lowell Club served) and certainly not "dainty" as some men of the time might have expected.[14] Indeed, the quantity of the food served would have satisfied the hungriest male lawyer: fruit, soup, salad, a fish course, lamb, capon, and multiple desserts (but no cigars or cigarettes). Like the Kansas City School of Law event, the dinner was accompanied by a program, one far more serious than later offered in Kansas City. The speeches covered such topics as "Our Professional Sisters," "A World of Equal Suffrage," "The Woman Judge," and "The Woman's Legal Education Society." In spite of the sober nature of the after-dinner speeches, the program included a mock judicial order:

> ORDERED, that jollity with good fellowship be observed by all until this occasion shall have passed into history.

---

14 On "dainty" foods, *see* Freedman, *supra* note 10, at 110–11.

MENU

∞

Fruit Cocktail

∞

Consomme Belvue
Mixed Olives

∞

Half Fried Chicken

Escalloped Potatoes   Peas

∞

Lettuce with Thousand Island Dressing

∞

Ice Cream
Assorted Cakes

∞

Demi Tasse

Cigars
Cigarettes

Kansas City School of Law
Washington's Birthday Banquet
1929

The menu for the 1929 Washington's Birthday Banquet of the Kansas City Law School was more modest in its offerings and in its messaging than that of the Lowell Club, featuring fewer delicacies and far more Midwestern in what was on offer: fruit cocktail instead of oysters and half fried chicken rather than roast duckling. Nevertheless, a whiff of Paris is present in the "consommé Belvue."[15] But though the food was less elaborate, the level of conviviality was certainly not. The dinner featured multiple toasts to such people as "women of the revolutionary period," "the new patriotism," and "our lawyer patriots," as well as an address by the local Federal District Judge, a presentation of the class picture, and dancing to follow. No doubt this was a memorable occasion, precisely why one of the attendees saved his menu as a keepsake.

24th Annual Washington's Birthday BANQUET

Kansas City School of Law
COLONIAL BALL ROOM
HOTEL MUEHLEBACH
FEBRUARY 22,
1929

---

15 Consommé Belvue (note the correct spelling) is a soup made from chicken stock, clam juice, cayenne pepper, and heavy cream; see *Consomme Bellevue*, IFoodTV (Jan. 4, 2012) https://ifood.tv/soup/410513-consomme-bellevue. This soup was also served at the Biltmore Hotel in New York City in November 1917. A bowl cost $0.45, second in cost only to the turtle soup with Amontillado Sherry. *Menus*, NEW YORK PUBLIC LIBRARIES, http://menus.nypl.org/menu_pages/67725/explore.

Menu

⌁ ⌁ ⌁

HORS D'OEUVRES, FINANCIERE

CLEAR GREEN TURTLE, AMONTILLADO
TOASTED BUTTER CRUSTS

CELERY   QUEEN OLIVES   NUTS
RIPE JUMBO OLIVES STUFFED WITH PIMENTOS

AIGUILETTE OF NEW ORLEANS POMPANO, SAUTE MEUNIERE
CUCUMBERS

ORANGE SHERBERT

SUPREME OF YOUNG CAPON, VIRGINIENNE, FRESH MUSHROOMS
SAUSE PERIGEUX
POMMES PARISIENNE   NEW GREEN STRING BEANS

COMBINATION FRUIT SALAD
PARMESAN CHEESE STRAWS   FRENCH DRESSING

BOMBE GLACE, SPECIAL
PETITS FOURS   MIGNARDISES

DEMI TASSE

The 53rd Annual Dinner of the American Bar Association

1930

The American Bar Association has long been the largest and most powerful professional legal group in the United States. It sees itself as the "face of the Law" in this country. It also holds an annual meeting that attracts lawyers from across the nation and features speeches, educational programs, and social gatherings, including splendid meals. On 22 August 1930, in the midst of the Great Depression, the ABA hosted its Annual Meeting Dinner in Chicago, and it was spectacular. The meal began with hors d'oeuvres and Green Turtle soup, a fish course of pompano, and a meat course of "young capon," with side dishes, salad, and desserts. Nearly all of the dishes were French (or at least their names were French). Instead of speeches, the program consisted of musical selections including Elgar's *Pomp and Circumstance* and selections from the popular musical *Show Boat*. The message was clear to anyone who attended the dinner or read the menu and program: even amidst the struggles of the Great Depression, the American Bar was doing just fine!

MENU

SUPREME OF FRUIT FLORIDA

———

CHICKEN MULLIGATAWNY

———

CELERY   OLIVES   RADISHES

———

ROAST YOUNG ANNE ARUNDEL CO. TURKEY

GOLDEN DRESSING

NEW GARDEN PEAS

CANDIED SWEET POTATOES

CRANBERRY SAUCE

———

ASPARAGUS TIP SALAD
FRENCH DRESSING

———

PUMPKIN PIE   AMERICAN CHEESE

———

LARGE COFFEE

———

MINTS

Dinner for William H. Lawrence by
the Bar and Laity of Baltimore, Maryland [16]
1936

The dinner given in 1936 in honor of William Lawrence stands out as one in which the chef decided to feature a local main dish: "Roast Young Anne Arundel County" turkey accompanied by peas, sweet potatoes, and cranberry sauce. It took place on October 16, so it would seem that the menu was intended to be a foreshadowing of the upcoming Thanksgiving holiday.[17] The pumpkin pie for dessert would appear to confirm this. It was certainly a classic American menu since it also featured "Supreme of Fruit Florida," although an exotic note was added by the presence of mulligatawny soup. Other than the French dressing, the good people of Baltimore seem to have stayed away from Francophile notes in the food. The program lists neither toasts nor speeches, but does mention after dinner dancing, which indicates that both men and women were present.

---

16 William H. Lawrence was a prominent Maryland lawyer who was appointed Baltimore County Circuit judge in 1936. The appointment was not without controversy; see, Jeff Scholnick, *Q: What Baltimore County Circuit Court Judge Stepped Down, Was Reappointed Within 5 Days & Later Won Election to the Bench? A. The Honorable William H. Lawrence,* BALTIMORE COUNTY SMALL AND SOLO ATTY'S BLOG (2010) https://baltimorecountysmallandsoloatty.wordpress.com/2010/09/19/q-what-baltimore-county-circuit-court-judge-stepped-down-was-reappointed-within-5-days-later-won-election-to-the-bench-a-the-honorable-william-h-lawrence/

17 The dinner also came just a few weeks before Lawrence was appointed to the Bench on November 9. One might also speculate that the "comfort food" aspect of the dinner was related to Lawrence's Republican political affiliations (shared with the Governor who appointed him and attended the dinner). He was the first Republican appointed to the Bench since the Civil War. *Id.*

MENU
o   o

Lobster and Crabmeat Louis

Key West Turtle Soup
Golden Cheese Straws

Hearts of Celery   Ripe and Green Olives
Salted Nuts

Breast of Native Guinea Hen Virginia
Wild Rice   New String Beans

Glace Surprise   Petit Fours

Demi Tasse

Dinner for Thomas Dewey by the Columbia Law School Alumni Association
1947

The American Bar has always been quite enthusiastic about honoring its successful members with speeches, eulogies, and celebrations of notable achievements. In 1947 the Alumni Association of the Columbia Law School put on a splendid feast at the Waldorf-Astoria in honor of Thomas Dewey, then Governor of the State of New York and an often talked about Presidential hopeful. The menu was fitting for an American political icon: lobster and crabmeat to start, followed by Key West turtle soups, and "breast of native guinea hen Virginia." There was a hint of French elegance (crabmeat "Louis" and "glace surprise"), but for the most part the dinner was solidly American. There was a toastmaster—and presumably toasts—and speeches by the President of the university, the Dean of the law school, a federal judge, the N.Y.C. district attorney, and of course, by the honoree, Governor Dewey. Although putatively a law school alumni event, there can be little doubt that the dinner featured a great deal of political networking.

Menu

◇

VINS	
	Le Cantaloup Rafraichi
	────
Fine Old Manzinella	La Tortue Claire au Xérès
	Les Paillettes D'or
────	────
	La Darne de Saumon d'Ecosse Pochée
Batard Montrachet 1949	Sauce Béarnaise
	Pommes Nouvelles
────	────
	Le Suprême de Volaille en Aspic
Charles Heidsieck 1949	La Salade Princesse
────	────
	Les Belles Framboises Melba
	Les Petits Fours
Croft 1935	
	────
Camus "Hors d'Age"	Le Mocha Royal

The Law Society Counsel Dinner
1957

The Law Society of England and Wales is the professional organization for solicitors and its Council is its governing body. Thus, a dinner put on for such an august gathering must be of the highest caliber. Once again, the dishes are all named in French and the food itself is quite spectacular: turtle soup, Scottish salmon, and a Supreme de Volaille in aspic. Notably, the menu also includes the wines provided to accompany each course, including an old Manzanilla sherry for the turtle soup, a 1949 Batard Montrachet, a 1949 Charles Heidsieck champagne, a 1935 vintage port, and an old Camus cognac to finish off the splendid meal. From start to finish, this dinner was produced with the highest artistry. My copy of the menu has the engraved copy of the invitation inserted in it. It is a masterpiece of the printer's art. One particularly telling note on the invitation to the dinner is that there will be no speeches. The guests could enjoy each other's company and the brilliant food, but would not be forced to endure endless speeches. One may assume by the prominent place in which this note appears that the lack of speeches was believed to be an additional inducement to attendance!

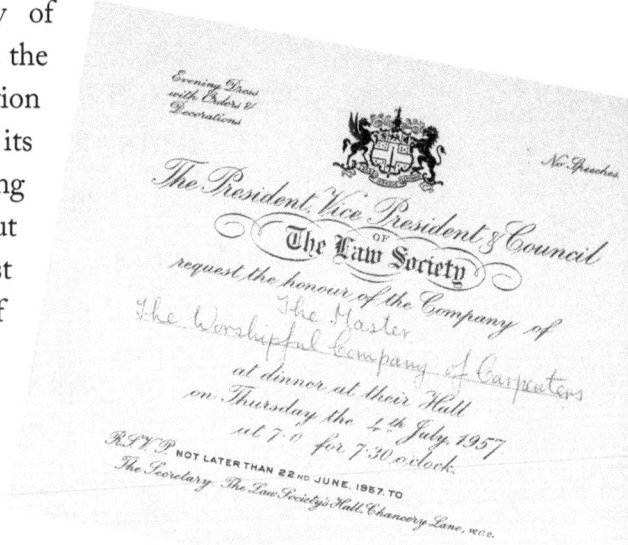

CRAVATH, SWAINE & MOORE

DINNER DANCE

MENU

Château Carbonnieux   Petite Marmite Henri IV
(Graves)
1975
                              *

Saumon Pôché, Sauce Hollandaise
Concombres Braisés

*

Château Selle de Veau Rôti, Sauce à l'Estragon
Pichon-Longueville,   Courgettes Florentine
Comtesse de Lalande   Carottes aux Fines Herbes
(Pauillac)
1971
                              *

Salade de Saison au Citron
Fromage de Brie

*

Praline Glacée aux Pêches Flambées

Café

January 12, 1980   The Pierre

The Cravath Annual Dinner Dance
1980

The final menu pictured here is one that I had the good fortune to enjoy as an associate at Cravath, Swaine & Moore. Although I had attended many an elegant banquet in my life before this, both in England as a Research Fellow at Cambridge and then as a young lawyer at Cravath, the January 12 dinner dance held at the Pierre Hotel in New York stands out even more than four decades later as one of the best culinary and convivial experiences of my life. The food, all named in French on the menu, and the wines were of the highest quality. As a dinner dance both sexes were present and I remember seeing—for the first time—many of my colleagues, male and female and their spouses, dressed far more elegantly than was customary in our daily routines. It was also one of the few times during the year when associates and partners were able to enjoy an informal and convivial meal together away from the pressures of work.[18]

---

18 The firm also sponsored a summer outing each year to which all the lawyers were invited. The food at these summer outings was quite good, but not so elegant as at the dinner dance.

A FEW RECIPES TO TRY FROM THE FEASTS

For those of you who have read the menus in this chapbook and wondered what it would be like to sample some of the dishes contained therein, I include here a few recipes. Some of the recipes are drawn from vintage cookbooks in my personal culinary library and online sources, others are my own. Try them at your risk!

DINNERS READY !

ALOYAU DE BŒUF ROTI AU CRÈME DE RAIFORT
(Sirloin of roast beef in horseradish sauce)

*Served at the retirement dinner by the Bar of Scotland
for Lord Shand.*

Although the French name suggests a complex dish, essentially the diners were served roast beef in a horseradish sauce. There are as many ways of cooking roast beef as there are cooks. I favor my grandmother's method, which produces a very rare meat. First, I brine the beef and, once this is done, I cover the beef in Kosher salt, ground pepper, and garlic powder. I roast it in the oven at 350° F for 10-15 minutes per pound, basting occasionally. Then I take it out of the oven and let it rest for ten minutes. When rested I slice the beef thinly and serve with horseradish sauce. This is available commercially or can be made easily from grated horseradish, sour cream, mayonnaise, Dijon mustard, and salt and pepper. Proportions are up to you; just go easy on the grated horseradish. It can be quite hot.[19]

TURTLE SOUP IN ALL ITS VERSIONS

Many of the menus feature a version of turtle soup. Below are recipes for two versions printed in The Presidential Cookbook *(1904), pp. 32-33. They are purely for reading and not reproduction, as green turtles are a protected species in the U.S. and their consumption is illegal.*

Mock Turtle Soup, of Calf's Head

Scald a well-cleansed calf's head, remove the brain, tie it up in a cloth, and boil an hour, or until the meat will easily slip

---

19 For an interesting account of how to cook roast beef in the French manner, see, The Everyday French Chef recipe online at everydayfrenchchef.com.

from the bone; take out, save the broth; cut it in small, square pieces, and throw them into cold water; when cool, put it in a stewpan, and cover with some of the broth; let it boil until quite tender, and set aside.

In another stewpan melt some butter, and in it put a quarter of a pound of lean ham, cut small, with fine herbs to taste; also parsley and one onion; add about a pint of the broth; let it simmer for two hours, and then dredge in a small quantity of flour; now add the remainder of the broth, and a quarter bottle of Madeira or sherry; let all stew quietly for ten minutes and rub it through a medium sieve; add the calf's head, season with a very little cayenne pepper, a little salt, the juice of one lemon, and if desired, a quarter teaspoonful pounded mace and a dessert-spoon sugar.

Having previously prepared force-meat balls, add them to the soup five minutes after serve hot.

Green Turtle Soup

One turtle, two onions, a bunch of sweet herbs, juice of one lemon, five quarts of water, a glass of Madeira.

After removing the entrails, cut up the coarser parts of the turtle meat and bones. Add four quarts of water, and stew four hours with the herbs, onions, pepper and salt. Stew very slowly, do not let it cease boiling during this time. At the end of four hours strain the soup, and add the finer parts of the turtle and the green fat, which has been simmered one hour in two quarts of water. Thicken with brown flour; return to the soup-pot, and simmer gently for an hour longer. If there are eggs in the turtle, boil them in a separate vessel for four hours, and throw into the soup before taking up. If not, put in force-meat balls; then the juice of the lemon, and the wine; beat up at once and pour out.

Some cooks add the finer meat before straining, boiling all together five hours; then strain, thicken, and put in the green fat, cut into lumps an inch long. This makes a handsomer soup than if the meat is left in.

Green turtle can now be purchased preserved in air-tight cans.

Force Meat Balls for the Above.—Six tablespoonfuls of turtle-meat chopped very fine. Rub to a paste, with the yolk of two hard-boiled eggs, a tablespoonful of butter, and, if convenient a little oyster liquor. Season with cayenne, mace, and half a teaspoonful of white sugar and a pinch of salt. Bind all with a well-beaten egg; shape into small balls; dip in egg, then powdered cracker; fry in butter, and drop into the soup when it is served.

LETTUCE WITH THOUSAND ISLAND DRESSING

*Served at Washington's Birthday Banquet at
the Kansas City Law School.*

To begin, Thousand Island Dressing is not Russian Dressing. There are many variations of Thousand Island dressing, but the basic recipe that I use includes a cup of mayonnaise, 3 tablespoons of ketchup, sweet green relish and chili sauce to taste (I use Tiger Sauce) to which I add a small amount of garlic, chopped hard-boiled egg (for thickening), and a few drops of Worcestershire sauce. One of the fun things about Thousand Island dressing is its history. I recommend reading the brief article by Jenifer Morrisey online at https://homeinthefingerlakes.com/homemade-1000-island-dressing/.

EGG MAYONNAISE

*Served at the River Thames Dinner Party at the
American Bar Association Convention.*

When I first arrived in Cambridge as a Fulbright in 1973, I was delighted to discover that students were expected to eat in the college hall for a formal dinner with some regularity. Although a bit more expensive than the college buttery (cafeteria), I loved putting on a gown, sitting at the long wooden tables, and having foods that I had never before tasted. One of my favorites was cold egg mayonnaise. Although there are many versions of this dish, my college (Clare) favored a very traditional recipe: a hard-boiled egg cut in half, covered with a mayonnaise sauce. Although I have never been able to pry the recipe from the chef at Clare, I tend to use one printed in *Recipes for High-Class Cookery as Used in the Edinburgh School of Cookery* (n.d.), p. 180:

Mayonnaise Sauce

2 yolks of eggs.	1 gill salad oil. [20]
Pepper, salt.	Vinegar.
A little mustard.	

Put the yolks and seasonings into a basin, and stir in the salad oil drop by drop. When thick and smooth stir in the vinegar.

For a more modern recipe, I recommend Melissa Clark's version on the *New York Times* Cooking page, online at https://cooking.nytimes.com/recipes/12459-mayonnaise.

SWEETBREAD CROQUETTES

Served at the Darke County Bar Association Banquet.

I am not a great fan of sweetbreads, so I include here the recipe for this dish from the Evaporated Milk Association's 1939 publication *Quality Recipes for Quantity Foods*[21]:

---

20 1 gill equals one-half cup. Vinegar to taste.

21 Accessed via *Public Domain Recipes* online at https://publicdomainrecipes.org/recipes/sweetbread-croquettes/

SWEETBREAD CROQUETTES
Yield: 100 croquettes

2½ cups butter (1¼ lbs)	Paprika
5 cups flour	3 tablespoons lemon juice
1¼ quarts hot chicken broth or water	10 pairs sweetbreads and chopped, cooked chicken to make 3¾ quarts
1¼ quarts evaporated milk	Fine bread crumbs
20 eggs	Evaporated milk
Salt	

Prepare a thick sauce of the butter, flour, broth or water and milk. Add beaten eggs, salt and paprika, then the lemon juice. Have the sweetbreads prepared in the following way: soak in cold water for 1 hour, renewing water several times. Simmer about 30 minutes in salted water to which ½ cup vinegar has been added. Rinse in cold water. Remove all membrane. Chop fine. Add chicken and combine with the sauce. Cool mixture and shape into croquettes. Roll in fine crumbs, then in undiluted evaporated milk and again in crumbs. Fry in deep fat (390° F) hot enough to turn a 1-inch cube of soft bread a golden brown in 40 seconds. Drain on unglazed paper to absorb excess fat. Serve on hot platter garnished with watercress.

If you have not eaten sweetbreads before, you might want to cut down the recipe from 100 croquettes to a smaller number on the first try.

CHICKEN MULLIGATAWNY

Served at the dinner for William H. Lawrence by the Bar and Laity of Baltimore. This soup was quite popular during the nineteenth and early twentieth centuries. Here are two recipes:

Potage à la Mulligatawney
From the *Presidential Cookbook*, p. 31

Fry in 1 tablespoonful butter, 1 tablespoonful fine-cut or chopped onion, the same of raw smoked ham, and green pepper; cook 5 minutes; then add the fine-cut breast of a young chicken, 2 tablespoonfuls fine-cut carrot, the same of white turnip and leeks; cook and stir 5 minutes; season with 1 teaspoonful salt, ½ teaspoonful pepper, 1 even teaspoonful curry; cover with 2 quarts chicken broth, prepared from the remaining chicken; add ½ cupful fine-cut egg-plant, ½ cupful fine-cut green apple, ¼ cup well-washed rice; boil 40 minutes; add, if necessary, more salt, and serve. In case the soup should be too thick, add more broth.

Clear Mulligatawney
From *Recipes for High-Class Cookery*

1 quart first stock.	1 onion.
4 oz. juicy beef.	1 small carrot.
1 gill of water.	½ apple.
1 white and shell of egg.	Salt.
1 tablespoon curry powder.	Lemon juice.
1 teaspoon curry paste.	*Garnish.*—2 oz. cooked chicken.

Shred the beef, and mix it with the water; add to it the curry powder and paste; soak for fifteen minutes. Put all ingredients into a clean saucepan. Whisk till almost boiling. Simmer for thirty minutes, and strain. Reheat; add the chicken cut in dice, and serve with dry rice.

A modern recipe I recommend may be found online at *The Wanderlust Kitchen*, https://thewanderlustkitchen.com/indian-mulligatawny-soup/.

∾

Some Final Thoughts

On my first day at Yale Law School, the late, great Geoffrey Hazard spoke at our class first day orientation about civility and proper behavior at the Bar. He concluded his inspiring talk with an admonition. He told the assembled new students that we should always remember that no matter how adversarial we might be in a courtroom setting, once we had left the courthouse precincts we should immediately abandon all aggressive and adverse behavior and wholeheartedly embrace our legal brethren. Indeed, he suggested that a visit to a local pub or eatery with our courtroom adversaries would be most advisable because we would quickly find that other lawyers would be the only people who would, in fact, want to join us for drinks or a meal. In this—as in so many things—Professor Hazard was correct. Public perceptions of lawyers have never been overly positive. Ours is a difficult profession that demands time and hard work and most often involves confrontational and adversarial behavior. Lawyers as human beings require more than this. Commensality and conviviality offer opportunities to bond on both a personal and professional level and permit us to relax amongst others who live similar lives. May the dinners long continue!

DINNERS READY!

www.ingramcontent.com/pod-product-compliance
Lightning Source LLC
Chambersburg PA
CBHW022035190326
41519CB00010B/1724